A Snake-Lover's Diary

BARBARA BRENNER

A Snake-Lover's Diary

ILLUSTRATED WITH PHOTOGRAPHS

Young Scott Books

Copyright 1970 by Barbara Brenner.
All Rights Reserved.
Young Scott Books
A Division of Addison-Wesley Publishing Company, Inc.
Reading, Massachusetts 01867
ISBN: 0-201-09349-9
Library of Congress Catalog Card No. 79-98113
Printed in the United States of America
Designed by William R. Scott

ACKNOWLEDGMENTS

A book always owes its life to many people besides the author. My son Mark's interest in snakes originally sparked the idea for this book. Carl, my younger son, was the literary and actual model for the boy in the story. Beyond my family, I owe a great debt of gratitude to Carl Kauffeld, Director and Curator of Reptiles, Staten Island Zoo, who not only read this manuscript but made many valuable suggestions and contributions. I also wish to thank Ray Van Nostrand, who supplied many of the specimens photographed here, and John Kenney, Nelson Bates, and Frederick Lewis of the staff of Bear Mountain Zoo, who assisted the photographer. There is no weighing the help I received from the enthusiastic band of amateur "herps" in Rockland County, especially Paul Folley and Josh Schwartz. Lastly, I'm extremely grateful to my friend George Ancona for his beautiful series of photographs.

B. B.

CONTENTS

1. April: Specimen A

I may as well begin by telling the reason for this diary. I've started it because of something special that happened today. It was when I was taking Shalom for his afternoon walk down in that old farm field. The two of us were walking along, enjoying all the signs of spring, when Shalom's good old retriever nose caught a whiff of something. He high-tailed it over to a log and began sniffing and digging around it. I didn't see anything, but knowing Shalom's nose, I figured something had to be there. So I picked up one end of the log and looked under it. There, coiled tightly in a little ring, was a Garter Snake.

I reached down and picked it up. It hardly moved. Just stayed in my hand, still groggy from its long

April 17

winter sleep. I turned it over and over, looking at the even white stripes that ran along its tan body, and the two small, perfect yellow dots on its head.

Now, I've seen snakes before. Even caught some. But somehow, this one was different. Maybe it was suddenly coming on something alive after the deadness of winter. Anyway, it was as if I'd never *really* seen a snake before. I decided then and there to take it home.

With Shalom bounding at my heels, I headed for the house. On the way, the plan began to take shape. I decided that I'd start a scientific study of snakes, and keep a diary of my findings. The Garter Snake would be my first specimen. I promptly named him Specimen A.

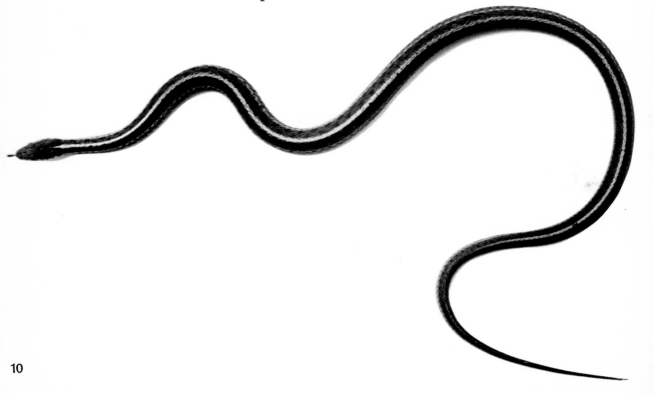

I stepped through the door, and ran smack into my first obstacle — Mom. "What is *that?*" she demanded.

"It's only a snake."

"Only a snake," she snorted. "I hate snakes."

"But it's a Garter Snake. They're harmless," I protested.

Mom was firm. She said she didn't care what kind of snake it was, she was not going to give it house room.

It looked as if my great plan was going to fail before I even got it off the ground. I put the snake in a jar so my mother would be less nervous, and then I sat down to try to convince her that she ought to let me keep snakes.

I explained my idea to her in detail. She said nix on snakes. I asked her where she had got her dislike of snakes. She said from the *Book of Genesis.* I said I didn't think it was nice of her to use the Bible to back up a prejudice. We talked for a while and she finally admitted that when she thinks of snakes she's really thinking of *poisonous* snakes. I told her that most snakes aren't poisonous, and that only a few venomous species live here in the northeast, the Copperhead and the Timber and Massasauga Rattlesnakes.

"What about the poisonous snakes who don't know their geography?" she wanted to know. I swore to her that snakes hardly ever move out of their territory. She seemed reassured, so I brought the jar a little closer. I told her again that this snake was absolutely harmless.

Then I gave her a short lecture on how beneficial snakes are. I said to her, "Do you realize that if it weren't for snakes we'd be up to our necks in rats and mice?" I told her something which the science teacher had told us. "Take a single pair of breeding field mice. If nothing ate any of their offspring," I quoted, "at the end of one year you'd have 1,200,000 field mice! Just think about that," I added, for dramatic effect.

The prospect of being overrun by field mice did not seem to shake Mom. She said she'd be happy to leave that problem to the cats and owls. Then I took the next step. I held the snake out to her. "Just touch it," I said. "You'll see. It isn't even slimy."

She touched it. "You're right," she said. "It isn't even slimy. But I still don't like it."

I was getting desperate. Everything depended on her accepting snakes. Just then Dad and Timmy came in. As soon as they understood the situation, they came to my rescue. The three of us managed to convince Mom that in the name of science, and to preserve her reputation as a good sport and super mother, she had to let me start a reptile collection.

She agreed, with the understanding that the snakes would all be kept in tanks with good tight-fitting covers. It was a deal.

So here I am in my bedroom. In front of me on the desk is our old aquarium tank. In it is my first specimen, an Eastern Garter Snake, eighteen inches long. Specimen A. Dad helped me set him up in here. Even helped me rig up a light bulb to keep him warm these chilly spring nights. "Because snakes are cold-blooded," Dad said. I never really understood before about that cold-blooded business. I always pictured some sort of refrigerator making their blood cold. It means they don't have an inner heating system, the way we do. Temperature goes down outside, their temperature drops. If it's warm outside, their body temperature rises.

Sounds rough. Forever at the mercy of the elements. The only thing a snake can do is to move. Out of the heat or into it. And if it gets too cold? Down under the ground to hibernate, I guess. So that's what cold-blooded is about.

Well, tomorrow I begin my study of snakes.

Today Dad and I went to the bookstore and bought **April 18** *A Field Guide to Reptiles and Amphibians,* by Roger Conant. No snake collector should be without it, the man in the bookstore said. It is a very complete book, has pictures and descriptions of every snake, lizard, frog, toad, or turtle that lives in the eastern part of the United States and Canada. (If you live out West, you get the *Field Guide to Western Reptiles and Amphibians.*)

Dad says I ought to start off right. He explained to me that all biology has a system of classification, and every organism has its place in it. Everything is classified according to its Kingdom, Phylum, Class, Order, Family, Genus, and Species. It seems like a lot to remember, but Dad taught me a little device that helps: King Philip Can Order Five Great Specimens. The first letter of every word gives you the key.

Here's how it works: Suppose you want to classify my Garter Snake. He belongs to the *Animal* Kingdom, and the Phylum *Chordata,* Subphylum *Vertebrata* (animals with a backbone). His Class is *Reptilia,* which simply means he's a reptile. He belongs to the Order *Squamata,* along with lizards; his Suborder *Serpentes,* separates him from the lizards. Next, the Garter Snake is one of the *Colubridae* family of snakes, a grouping which includes two-thirds of the world's snake population. His genus is *Thamnophis,* which tells that he's a kind of Garter Snake. Species tells exactly what type of Garter Snake he is, *sirtalis sirtalis. Sirtalis sirtalis* indicates that he was the first of the *sirtalis* species to be described. Any other subspecies of the *sirtalis*-type Garter Snake would have the word *sirtalis* followed by its subspecies name. Phew! I'm glad I have this diary; otherwise, I'd never remember all this.

To make it simple, you usually use the last two classifications, once it's clear you're talking about snakes. So Garter Snake is simply *Thamnophis sirtalis sirtalis.* (I may stick to calling him Specimen A!)

Timmy caught a Spring Peeper today. He says it's for my reptile collection. I tried to explain to him that a frog is an amphibian, not a reptile, and that we are only collecting reptiles. But he has already named

April 19

it Specimen B, and put it in a big pickle jar with holes in the lid for air, and a branch to climb on. So I guess we'll have to keep it.

It *is* sort of a nice little frog. I've never seen one up close before. It's only about an inch long, which probably makes it one of the smallest frogs you can find around here. And it can walk right up the side of that pickle jar without slipping!

Dad told Tim that he used to catch Spring Peepers when he was a kid. Tim was amazed. He said, "You mean they had the same kind of frogs when you were young?" My kid brother seems to think animals are like cars, and that Nature comes out with a new model every few years. Dad explained to him that a Spring Peeper has been a Spring Peeper for thousands of years. Tim couldn't believe it.

It's fun to watch that little frog puff out his throat when he chirps. Which he does all the time. Once he got used to his new home, he began "peep-peeping" away for dear life. Or maybe I should say for dear *wife;* that peep, according to the book, is his mating call. Mom thinks Tim ought to catch a mate for him. Poor Timmy. Those Spring Peepers are so hard to catch. "How will I tell the female from the male?" he wanted to know. Mom said she supposed he should look for a frog that's listening instead of peeping!

After school today I told Tim something about frogs, because he can't read real books yet. I told him there are frogs all over the world, wherever it's warm. Some of them live close to the water; others live in it. Most frogs come to the water to mate and lay their eggs. The word "amphibian" is Greek and means "living a double life." Their double life is that they don't hatch right out into frogs, but spend time being tadpoles first, and then become frogs. There are probably a half-dozen different kinds of frogs, right in our little backwoods pond. They stay around from spring until it gets cold. Then they go under the ground or into the pond mud for the winter.

April 20

The book says Spring Peepers eat live insects. So we spent the whole afternoon and evening catching live insects. It took us about two hours to collect ten garbage flies and a few early mosquitoes. We really worked up a sweat. Then when we went to put them into the jar something went wrong and—now there are ten garbage flies and a few early mosquitoes flying around the house. Mom is not too happy.

April 21   Today Tim and I caught a second batch of frog food. We turned the porch light on as soon as it got dark, and when the moths came flying toward the light, we just picked them off the screen door and collected them in a can. If I do say so myself, it was a brilliant idea of mine. This time we got them into the frog

jar without any accidents. You should see the way the Peeper went after them. One minute the moth was fluttering around in there. Then Specimen B saw it. His tongue shot out. Zap! The moth was gone. His tongue, by the way, is attached to the front of his mouth. If he flips it out, he turns it over completely. And fast. It takes less than a second for a Spring Peeper to flip his tongue out, land on target, and pop his victim down the hatch. And if you're not watching closely, you miss the whole show.

Meanwhile, the Garter Snake seems to be doing well. I haven't had a chance to do anything about getting food for him, but snakes normally may go without food for long periods of time. I'll get him something tomorrow.

And so to bed. I'm really pleased with the way the collection is growing. One reptile and one amphibian in less than a week. At this rate I could have sixteen specimens by the end of the summer.

April 22

Tragedy has struck. This morning when I looked for the Spring Peeper he was nowhere to be found. When I asked Timmy about it, he said he had taken him out of the jar and put him in the tank with the Garter Snake. Said he thought the frog looked lonesome! It never dawned on me to tell Tim about

Garter Snakes and frogs. But now he knows. There is no doubt about it. Specimen A has eaten Specimen B.

May 2   It's a week since Garter Snake came to live on my desk. The tank arrangement seems to be quite suitable for him. He has a dish of water big enough to drink from or climb into, a branch to climb on or rub against, and a good tight-fitting wire screen top on the tank, so he can't get out. At first there was nothing on the bottom of the tank. Now I've covered it with shredded newspaper, and I can just replace the newspaper when the snake soils it instead of having to wash the entire tank. Actually, I've discovered that snakes don't get rid of body wastes nearly as often as mammals do. Probably because they don't eat so often. Speaking of eating, I *know* what this snake likes to eat. Frogs and toads. He

Snake Tank with Corn Snake

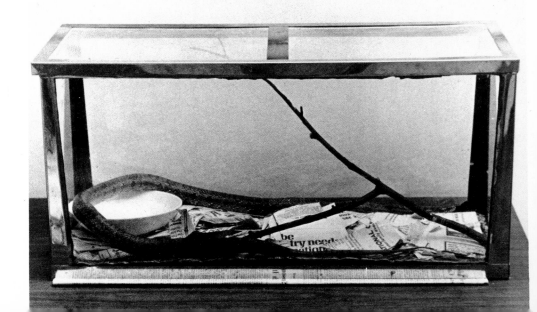

likes raw fish, too. Dad and I went fishing the other night and we gave him the insides of the fish after we cleaned them. He loved them.

This snake is perfectly gentle when he's handled properly. He doesn't like to be "dangled," and will try to bite me if I hold him by the tail. But if I hold him so that he has most of his body resting on my hand or arm, he'll move around on me in a very relaxed way.

Conclusions: A Garter Snake is a perfect pet. It's clean, easy to feed, and doesn't make any noise. It doesn't have to be walked, either!

May 3 "What's so special about snakes?" A kid asked me that today in school. I was so surprised that anyone would ask such a question that I was stumped for a minute, and before I could recover he went away. I hope I see him tomorrow because I've thought of some good answers. First I'm going to tell him that there are about 6,000 species of reptiles, including 2,700 kinds of snakes.

And I wonder if he knows that snakes have been around for about a million years. Their ancestors, the early lizards, go back maybe 250 million years. It seems to me that anything with a family tree *that* old is worth a closer look.

I'll get his curiosity aroused by telling him about the mystery surrounding the evolution of snakes. Scientists know that the earliest reptiles evolved from amphibians. They think that snakes may have come from a group of reptiles that lived under the ground, lost their legs, nearly lost their eyes and hearing, and then, much later, adapted again to a life above ground. But there the trail gets cold, because no one seems to know exactly why the snake took the shape it did. The only thing we do know is that snakes once had legs and then lost them. In fact, some of the most primitive snakes, like the Boa Constrictor, still have a leftover, or *vestigial* leg.

I'll bring up that vestigial leg as the final touch.

May 4

Mom is the only member of the family who still doesn't entirely appreciate my snake. She says she's not afraid of snakes any more, she just doesn't think they're very interesting.

"They're so dumb," she said the other day.

"Compared to what?" I snapped back.

"Well, for instance, a dog," she said. "Dogs are so much smarter."

The fact is, I love Shalom, and I wouldn't trade him for any animal. But a snake *is* unusual, and I think that's what appeals to me.

I said to her, "How many dogs do you know that can walk without legs, can eat something twice as big as they are, can hunt and find their food in the dark, can take care of themselves from the minute they are born, and," I said for a clincher, "can shed their skins every few months.

"Besides," I added, "if people chose their pets on the basis of intelligence, everyone would keep a chimpanzee. And look how many people keep tropical fish. They're no Einsteins either, if you come right down to it."

Mom laughed. "O.K., O.K., you win," she said. "Snakes have *charisma*." I looked up the word charisma in the dictionary. It means having a special power to attract people. That's just what snakes have. For me, anyway.

2. May: Collecting

I'm beginning to feel professional. Following the advice of the *Field Guide,* I've gotten myself a snake bag. This one is an old pillowcase, but actually, I could have used any sack made out of smooth fabric that wouldn't bruise a snake's skin or get caught on its scales. You can even use an old sock for small specimens. But—no holes. Snakes can get out of the tiniest opening. They have a way of flattening and elongating their bodies just for escape purposes. The nice thing about a bag is that you can knot it onto your belt and have both hands free for catching.

I've found a place I call the Sand Dunes. You'd never know it was there from the road. You come to a Water Company sign and there's a dirt road and you ride down it and then—all of a sudden you're on a hillside overlooking a field of marsh grass and sand and little puddles of water and beyond that — the river. Down here it's just a stream that moves through the reeds and over flat rocks and clumps of pickerel weed. Nobody seems to come here.

It looks like a perfect spot for Water Snakes, but I didn't see any today. Saw some other wildlife, though. A pair of ducks. A Green Heron. Redwing Blackbirds. Such a nice, quiet, peaceful place. Shalom thinks so, too.

May 22 My quiet, peaceful spot wasn't so quiet today. I went down there after school. As soon as I got to the river, I spotted a Water Snake on a log in the sun.

Water Snakes found around here aren't poisonous, so I felt free to take off my sneakers and wade into the water after this new specimen. Shalom came right with me; he went around one side of the log and I went around the other. Naturally, that snake wasn't going to sit there and wait for us to surround him. He slid into the water and just as he went under, I grabbed him. He was heavier than I thought, and before I knew it I'd slipped and sat right down on that gooey bottom. Clouds of mud came up all around me. I couldn't even *see* the snake but I still had hold of him. I slowly pulled myself out of the ooze, hanging on to the wriggling brown and black mass. When I finally staggered to my feet I was clutching four feet of slippery Water Snake. And was he mad! Before I could get to my snake bag, and stow him safely away, he bit me. I was more surprised than any-

thing when I looked down and saw him hanging onto my arm with his teeth.

Almost without thinking, I reached down and pried his teeth loose. Then, as I held him, I got another shock. He let me have it with secret snake weapon number two, a smelly, oily secretion from the gland at the base of his tail. All over my pants, my shirt, my hands. Ugh!

I really stunk when I got home. Shalom and I were sneaking in the back door to go into the basement when Mom appeared. She gasped. I guess we must have looked pretty awful, covered from head to foot with that black pond mud. Mom said, "Say something so I'll know which is the front of you."

I said, "I caught a Water Snake."

My mother said, "Or vice versa," and told me to go downstairs and take a shower.

I did. I washed the bite off and put some disinfectant on it. Then I went to take a look at my catch.

That Water Snake is beautiful. I'm keeping him in an old bathtub in the basement, temporarily. I've put a big piece of screen over the top. But I can see that I'm going to have to get some more tanks for my collection. I could build a wooden box for each specimen. Wooden boxes with wire mesh tops and fronts are pretty good containers for reptiles. A glass tank is even better, and easier to keep clean. I talked my plans over with Dad, and he said he'd come to the pet store with me and see what we could work out. I showed him the Water Snake and told him about the bite. We talked about the best way to grab a snake, which is just behind the head. I explained about getting him in the water.

May 23   Lucky break. The pet store is moving and the owner sold us ten old, leaky fish tanks. Big ones. They were really cheap, so we splurged and bought some aluminum paint. Dad and I washed and painted the rusty ones. That ought to solve the snake housing problem. Now I have two tanks and two snakes in my room. The rest of the tanks are in the basement, waiting for my next catch.

Personality traits: Garter Snake continues to be sweet-tempered and gentle. The Water Snake is more aggressive, but he has at least calmed down to the point where he doesn't squirt me with that awful musky stuff when I pick him up. Many snakes have this defense mechanism, including Garter Snakes. But Garter has never squirted me. I wonder why?

I read somewhere that snakes like to have a dark spot to crawl into. So I've given the Garter Snake a rock ledge to crawl under, and I made Water Snake a little house—a cardboard box with a hole in it. The box stands in the corner of the tank, but so far he hasn't used it. He lies in the water dish all day, and eats fish guts whenever I supply them. Keeping two snakes is not much more work than keeping one. I change the water every day, clean the tank paper when it needs it, and feed them once a week.

Guess who caught a snake today? Dad. He found it on an indoor tennis court, which is a pretty unlikely place to find a snake. We've identified it as a DeKay's Snake (after a naturalist named James Edward De-Kay) or Northern Brown Snake. It's one of the world's smallest snakes; this one is only seven inches long. Looks like a big worm, except that it has a snake's head. It seems silly to put DeKay all alone in one of those great big, new tanks. I'm going to put

May 25

him in with Garter Snake. It says in the book that Garter Snakes don't eat other snakes. (I'm learning to check these things!)

DeKay eats worms. Some of the nightcrawlers I put in there are bigger than he is, but he manages. Opens up his mouth and engulfs them. Those movable jaws that snakes have come in handy. They also have powerful saliva which helps with the job of digestion as soon as the food starts going down. The fact is, eating is one of the snake's big jobs, so he's designed to do it efficiently.

May 29   A real find today, at our friend's house in upstate New York—a Hognose Snake, sometimes called a "puff adder" or a "hissing adder." As soon as I saw

it, I recognized the upturned nose and the dark gray body. And the clownish ways! When we first came on him, he reared up, flattened his head, and began to hiss. He succeeded in terrifying Shalom, who jumped right up into the air, and wasn't seen for the rest of the afternoon. When Hognose saw that his fake cobra act wasn't going to scare the humans, he began to twitch and then suddenly stiffened and rolled over in a perfect imitation of sudden death. Dad took a stick and turned him right-side up. He immediately rolled right back again. What a performance!

We brought the Hognose Snake home in a damp snake bag, which we kept in the coolest part of the car so that he wouldn't get too hot and dry on the long trip. I've installed him in a tank all by himself. I went out and got him a live toad, which is what he's supposed to eat, but he didn't give it a second look. I hope he'll eat when he feels more at home.

June 4   So far, we have collected:

1 Eastern Garter Snake *Thamnophis sirtalis sirtalis*
1 Northern Water Snake *Natrix sipedon sipedon*
1 DeKay Snake *Storeria dekayi dekayi*
1 Eastern Hognose Snake *Heterodon platyrhinos*

Four different species from four different genera. All caught within two miles of the house, with the exception of Hognose.

It's hard to believe that just a few months ago, I thought all snakes looked alike. Seeing these four snakes together, I realize how different snakes are from one another. And yet these four all belong to the *Colubridae* family.

I guess the point is that most people don't really look at snakes. They're too busy running away from them. Having them here in my room gives me a good chance to observe. What do you see when you look hard at snakes? Their differences and their similarities. Observations:

All snakes are the same general shape. But some are long and skinny, others are stubby and fat. All snakes have scales, but even the scales vary. Water Snake, for instance, has broad, heavy scales, while DeKay's are delicate and tiny.

Snakes vary in color and size. So far, I have four snakes ranging from DeKay, who measures seven inches tip to tail, to Water Snake, who's a good four feet (but refuses to be measured), with Garter and Hognose somewhere between. In other places in the world, there are snakes that measure up to thirty feet long.

But big or small, there are some things that seem to be standard equipment on every snake. All snakes have two eyes, two nostrils, a mouth, a tongue, and two rows of teeth.

One of the first things that you notice about a snake's eyes is that they never blink. I thought at first that it was because they don't have any eyelids. They do, but their eyelids are transparent. A snake is forever looking out the window of his eyelids.

You can tell something about a snake from the shape of its eye. Round eyes belong to snakes that hunt in the day. Up-and-down eyes, like those of the

Boa and the Rattlers, usually belong to the night prowlers.

Snakes depend on their sense of smell to help them hunt. But they use their *tongues* to help them smell things. When you see a snake flick that forked tongue in and out of his mouth, he's taking a sample of the air. Then he throws it back against the roof of his mouth where a sensitive smell-taste detector called *Jacobsen's organ* sorts out the smells for him. This organ, together with his nose, helps him to track his prey and to sense danger.

A dentist would probably be interested in seeing a snake's teeth, which he doesn't use for chewing at all. There are two rows on each side of his upper jaw, one on each side of his lower jaw. And they all curve inward, like little hooks. Whatever he grabs, he can hold onto. Considering the fact that a snake has no arms or legs, no paws or claws, he has developed a perfect set of tools for gripping. And if he loses a tooth, another one will grow to replace the old one!

But the jaws of a snake are where the action is. A snake's jaws aren't joined together at the chin, the way ours are. Instead, they're barely connected, by a ligament. This makes his right and left jawbones, both upper and lower, movable units. He can actually "walk" his food into his mouth, by shifting his jaws back and forth. This, together with the fact that many of the bones of his skull can move, is the reason why a snake can manage to swallow prey that's often bigger than he is.

Speaking of food, I wish I knew why the Hognose Snake won't eat.

June 6   I notice that a milky film has come over Hognose's eyes. He spends hours curled up in his water dish. He looks terrible. What's the matter with him? Is he sick? Should I let him go?

June 8 The mystery of Hognose Snake has been solved. This morning about ten o'clock, he began to move his head back and forth in a peculiar way. Then he started to rub his face in the newspaper on the bottom of the tank. I thought at first he was looking for food. But then I noticed that the skin around his mouth was peeling. He began slithering back and forth on his branch, and as he moved, the skin began to pull back, as if he were taking a glove off. He was shedding!

For the next hour or so, he moved slowly out of his old skin. It took quite a while. The hardest part seemed to be getting rid of the last few inches of skin, which clung to his tail until he climbed into the water dish. That loosened it, and it came right off, a perfect, complete shed, right down to the eye cover-

ings. I've since found out that all snakes shed their skin. The time between sheds varies; if a snake is eating a lot and growing fast it may shed as often as every couple of months. Even older snakes who aren't growing any more will shed and get a new top layer of skin every so often. What does a snake shed look like? As if you made a paper-thin mold of the whole snake. I'm going to press it, dry it, and mount it on my bulletin board.

Hognose looks beautiful now. His new skin is bright, colorful and shiny. His eyes are clear and sparkling. He has a brand-new outer layer.

A couple of months ago, I wouldn't even have known that you could find a constrictor in the Northeastern United States. I'd have thought they were all down in the jungles of South America. But here I am, with a constrictor on my desk, Specimen Number 5—an Eastern Milk Snake *Lampropeltis doliata triangulum.*

June 10

I was walking along the road that leads down to the pond we call the Forty-Foot Hole, and I came to a metal highway sign that had been knocked over. I remembered that piles of metal, like rock piles and trash piles, are good places to catch snakes. It's nice and warm and dark under there, I thought to myself. I lifted a corner of the sign, pulled it up, and—there

was the most beautiful snake I've ever seen. It's
white, black, and a rusty red. Patterned like a piece
of Indian pottery. As soon as it sensed my presence,
it began to vibrate its tail like a rattlesnake, and the
sound of that tail hitting the dry grass sent the hairs
on Shalom's back straight up.

I knew what it *wasn't*—a Copperhead or a Rattler,
but I didn't know what kind of snake it was. While
I was trying to figure it out, the snake left. I had an
idea that he wasn't going to give up a nice, cozy spot
so quickly. So I went down to the pond, walked
around for a while, and then came back about an

hour later. Sure enough. When I lifted the sign, old snake was there again. And this time I was ready for him. I nabbed him behind the head and dropped him into my snake bag. That's how I got Milk Snake, the most nervous, high-strung and temperamental of my brood.

3. June: In the Field

I've finally met someone who likes snakes as much
as I do. His name is Buzz Allen, he's eighteen, and
he works at the Museum of Natural History. He
wants to be a *herpetologist,* which is a biologist who
specializes in reptiles and amphibians. "Herp" for
short.

 We met down at the Forty-Foot Hole. At first I
thought he was a fisherman, but then I saw his snake
stick and his collecting bag. We started to talk and
now we have a date to meet tomorrow.

Buzz and I meet down at the swamp. We go early or
at dusk, because those are the best collecting times.

June 12

June 17

Also because he has to go to work and I have to go to school, at least for another week.

Sometimes we pump up his rubber life raft and paddle downstream on the river. My favorite time is early in the morning, when the mist is rising, and there's no sound but the birdcalls and the splashes of the paddles in the water. That's when you feel it's just you and the animals, alone together.

There's a lot to being a "herp," and Buzz is teaching me some of the fine points. For instance, I was going after the snakes with my hands, or with a forked stick I whittled from a hickory limb. Buzz showed me how to make a real snake stick, out of an old golf club of Dad's. We filed it down and shaped it until it's just right for holding a snake behind the head, or lifting one to put it in a snake bag. I also use it to turn over logs and rocks. That way you don't use your hands and run the risk of getting bitten. Buzz says it's a good precaution, even if there are no poisonous snakes around. (You can run into a bees' nest poking around under logs!)

Speaking of logs, Buzz says not to step over a log. You never know what's on the other side. You should step onto it and look over. He also says you should always replace the environment when you're collecting. Don't overturn a log or rock and leave it. You may be destroying an animal's natural home.

Dad and Mom bought me a pair of high leather snake boots like the ones that Buzz has. They're great for tramping through brambles and muddy swamps, and besides, they're protection against an angry, poisonous snake that's been stepped on by mistake.

A SNAKE-LOVER'S DIARY

June 18 Buzz is going to take me with him on a collecting trip to the New Jersey Pine Barrens. Mom *has* to let me go!

June 20 I am seventy-five miles from home, lying in a sleeping bag writing by the beam of a flashlight. We're in the middle of what seems like complete wilderness. What a place! It's hard to believe that wide open spaces like this exist so near big cities. But here it is. Miles of flat open forest; sand and woods and scrubby little pine trees. Cranberry bogs and cedar swamps. And very few people. Buzz seems to know all the back roads that only his jeep can get through. We're camped in a spot I could never find again.

We got here about noon, took a swim in the clearest pond I've ever seen, and have spent the rest of the day exploring. There may not be many people here, but there's plenty of evidence of wild life. Deer tracks. Mink nests. And birds! There must be a hundred different kinds of birds in the Pine Barrens. We had a pair of towhees following us all afternoon. They hopped from tree to tree, calling and watching. We saw my old friends the Redwings, too. And a few ducks. Buzz says that sweet song we heard this evening is the Pine Warbler.

Of course, our main interest is to look for reptiles

and amphibians, and there are plenty here. We've already seen Leopard Frogs and Green Frogs, Spotted Turtles and a big Snapping Turtle. Buzz is going to try to show me a Pine Barren Treefrog, *Hyla andersoni*, which is a rare frog found here in the Pine Barrens and almost nowhere else.

Every time I move in the sleeping bag I hear the crunch of pine needles, and there's a nice smell in the air. . . . I'm going to remember this trip.

I suppose it had to happen sooner or later. Today I had a run-in with a rattlesnake.

June 21

We were tramping through a clearing at the edge of the woods, picking up loose lumber, turning over debris, and generally poking around with our snake sticks looking for specimens. It was a fine sunny morning and we were having a great time listening to the birds and crickets and the hundreds of other noises that make up the total sound of a wilderness place.

It was all these sounds that distracted me. When I heard a new high-pitched buzzing added to them, I didn't really think about it. Just about the time that I realized what it was, Buzz heard it and yelled "Rattler," and the snake struck. I felt a dull thud against my boot, and I looked down and saw a thin stream of yellowish liquid running down the leather. At the same time I saw a coiled Timber Rattlesnake. I had almost stepped on it!

Buzz was yelling to me and I guess I panicked. In a dream I watched myself raise the snake stick and bring it down right on the snake's neck. It didn't even twitch. In a second or two, Buzz was beside me.

The first thing he did was to look at my leg. "You're sure it didn't touch your leg?" he asked me. I was so scared I could only point to the wet spot on my boot and the two small fang marks in the leather.

Once he saw that I was all right, he exploded. "Don't you look where you're going? Didn't you hear it? You almost *stepped* on that snake, and now you've killed it." He said a couple of other things that I won't write here.

When Buzz finally calmed down he told me to go get some water and a rag and wash off my boot and not to let my hands touch the venom.

Buzz was bending over the dead snake. When I had pulled myself together, I joined him.

It was a small specimen, luckily for me. If this snake had been four or five feet long instead of its two-foot length, it might have reached my hand or arm instead of my boot. I felt weak thinking about it.

Buzz must have seen my white face. "Sit down," he said. "I'll give you a little lecture on poisonous snakes." We sat on a log in the sunshine and Buzz held the snake and told me about it.

"Rattlesnakes are pit vipers. See here—these pits on either side of his head. That's how he feels heat —the heat of a warm-blooded animal. When he strikes"—here Buzz stopped and forced the snake's mouth open with a stick—"the venom is piped from a gland back here"—he pointed to a spot below and behind the eye—"to these hollow teeth in front— and whammo! He gets his victim with a single bite. And then he just waits for it to die."

It all seemed a little hard to believe. That innocent-looking liquid that I'd taken off my boot? As if Buzz could read my thoughts he continued, "Venom is a pretty powerful chemical. It has some things in it which destroy the cells of the nervous system. Other substances attack the blood. And still others are like strong saliva—they break down tissues."

"How long does it take?" I asked, looking at all that dangerous equipment.

"Depends. A full-grown Timber Rattler could kill a rabbit in a few minutes."

"How long to kill a person?" I asked timidly. Buzz answered that it was possible for a person to die in a matter of hours from rattlesnake bite, but he added, "Don't forget that venom is primarily for the purpose of getting food. A Timber Rattlesnake won't go out of its way to strike at a human being. It only bites people as a defense. Anyway," he added, "more people are killed in the United States by lightning every year than by snakebite."

I got the distinct feeling that Buzz thought that anyone who *allowed* himself to get bitten by a rattlesnake was a super idiot. He took out his hunting knife and said, hardly bothering to conceal his disapproval, "As long as you've killed this snake we may as well save the skin." He proceeded to skin the snake. When he was finished he held it up. "Look here. See the rattles. Every time a rattler sheds he adds another segment. When the snake vibrates his tail, the dry links of horn hit together and make the rattling sound."

He handed me the skin. "Here," he said shortly. "Souvenir. Stretch it and dry it. Then put it on your wall to remind yourself to be more careful."

He turned his attention to what was left of the snake. "Let's see what he's been feeding on," he said, and opened the snake's stomach. Inside was a field mouse, half dissolved by those powerful digestive juices.

"How awful," I said.

"Why awful?" growled Buzz. "A snake has to live, too. And he kills his victims a lot more mercifully than most other creatures do. One bite and it's all over. Have you ever seen the way they kill the animals *you* eat?"

I went back to the car, feeling sick and foolish. Buzz must have realized how it was for me, because he was extra nice. He drove me into the nearby town.

We bought a few supplies, and I got some film for my camera. By the time we got back to our camp site I felt much better, cheerful enough to tell Buzz about the book I had just read on snake customs among primitive tribes. I informed him that if we had been natives of British New Guinea, we would have burned that snake and smeared its ashes on our legs to keep other poisonous snakes away for the rest of the trip.

June 22   Our last day, and still we haven't caught any snakes, except the Rattler. And we certainly didn't want him. Buzz is back in good humor although he says I've jinxed him because we're not seeing any snakes. Now I know why they call this place the *Barrens*. It certainly is. At least barren of snakes.

Important P.S. It was about four o'clock and we were packing up to come home, a little disappointed at our bad luck. We decided to take a last look around. I was looking through a mound of burned-out garbage and I spied a head among the cans and bottles. I took a quick look to make sure and then dove for it. I yelled for Buzz to give me a hand and together we reeled it in, like a rope. Buzz kept yelling, "It's a King, it's a King," and I just kept pulling until we got it all out. It was a Kingsnake , a beautiful, shiny black serpent with a creamy white chain pattern. It's sometimes called a "swamp wamper."

"You can *keep* him," said Buzz, and I didn't need a second invitation. I deposited him carefully in my snake bag, and now here I am at home. Number 6 has arrived: Kingsnake *Lampropeltis getulus getulus*. He is the same genus as the Milk Snake, which means he's also a constrictor.

4. July: A Square Meal

School is over. Hooray!

June 30

The one event guaranteed to win Mom over to snakes has happened. Garter Snake has given birth to seventeen babies. I thought that snake looked a little plump. But seventeen! I didn't even know she was *gravid*. (That's my new word for the day. It means pregnant.)

July 5

Most of the babies were born during the night, so we missed seeing the complete birth process. But we did see the last two snakes being born. They came out of an opening near the snake's tail, called the *vent*. It's the same opening through which the male snake fertilizes the female. Each baby snake was born covered with a thin membrane, which it broke through right away.

Throughout the part of the birth that we saw, Mama Garter didn't give her babies a second glance. I couldn't help but contrast her behavior with that of Lovelady, Shalom's mother. I remember how she washed the pups and nursed them and taught them things. Question: Is being "motherly" evidence of higher intelligence? Naturally, Mom says yes. I'm not so sure. I think maybe lower orders of animals operate more on instinct, and in higher orders, more behavior has to be taught by parents and learned by the young.

To think that I didn't know that Garter Snake was a female. On the other hand, even the experts say it's hard to tell a male snake from a female unless you have them side by side so you can compare tails. Then you can sometimes see that the male snake's tail is longer and thicker. That's because he has two sex organs called *hemipenes* in his tail. They carry the sperm to fertilize the female.

Not all snakes bear live young; some lay eggs. They may lay as many as hundreds of them, sometimes stuck together in clusters. These eggs hatch after about eight weeks. Some snakes coil about their eggs, brooding them like birds do. The Indian Python, for instance, can even raise its body

temperature to help incubate its eggs, which is pretty interesting, considering that snakes are cold-blooded creatures. Timmy wants to know how you take a snake's temperature. Now there's a question!

Anyway, the babies have opened up a whole new world for Mom. She watches them. She picks them up. She brings all her friends in to see them. I even saw her out in the vegetable garden, digging worms for the little darlings. Things have sure changed around here.

We're going to let the baby snakes go. There's no **July 12** sense in keeping them. We've seen them. We've studied them. I even took pictures of them. Have to practice a little conservation.

True to snake form, Mrs. Garter has absolutely no

interest in her children. They could be in the gravest danger and she wouldn't lift a finger. Or should I say she wouldn't give a flick of her tongue?

July 15   Today was my birthday. By way of celebration, I decided to let the Garter babies go. Mom said good-bye to them, and I slipped them into a bag and put them in my bicycle basket.

I thought I'd release them in their ancestral home, which, I figured, was the middle of the old farm field where I had found their mother.

It was a beautiful day, so I spent a little time looking around, stalling, before I let them go. I noticed that the Mourning Cloak and Swallowtail Butterflies were out, looking for a free meal in the flowers. And the Redwings were bright black and red spots all over the field. I even saw a hawk wheeling around overhead. Looking for field mice, I thought to myself.

When I'd prolonged the moment as much as I could, I opened the bag, and emptied the wriggling cargo onto the path. I knew they'd take off in all directions into the brush. I started to walk away, my duty done. About fifty feet along, I turned around to see if they were gone yet. What I saw made me freeze stone-still on the meadow path.

It was the hawk, dive-bombing right toward the spot where I'd released the baby snakes. A moment later it plunged into a clump of milkweed. There was a slight rustling, then up it came and took off. But not before I spotted a small jerking rope in its talons. One of the baby snakes!

What a jackass, I thought to myself. You saw the hawk. Why didn't you realize it would eat the snake? One down. Sixteen left. Riding home, I thought of all the other things that could happen to the snakes. What were their chances for survival? How many would live to grow up in that small corner of the country?

They'd have to watch out for cats. Owls, too. A hawk could get another of them, and there were always hungry skunks. But what about their other enemies—I passed a dead snake on the road—cars! Lots of snakes come onto the highways at night and are hit by cars. And then there are the farmers, and hunters, and picnickers, who don't know a Garter Snake from a Copperhead or a Rattler, and just step on or stone a snake as a matter of course. A snake's life, I concluded, is not a very secure one. I wondered how many snakes live the twenty to thirty years which is considered the maximum life span of a snake in captivity.

And supposing they do live, I thought. What will they do with themselves? Most of a snake's time is taken up with the basic necessities. Looking for food, catching it and eating it is a standard snake occupation. So is finding and mating with another snake once a year, to insure the fact that snakedom will go on. Or maybe looking for a burrow, or a winter home. It would be interesting if you could follow a snake from its infancy to adulthood, and see just how it spends its time. Now *that* would be a good field study.

July 16 Buzz has gone to Mexico, where he is going to work for a man from the museum, doing some snake research. He had no place to leave his Kingsnake and his Boa, and since he'll be going to college in the fall, he has given them both to me. The Kingsnake is a Florida Kingsnake *Lampropeltis getulus floridana,* somewhat different from the Kingsnake I got in the Barrens. And the Boa Constrictor—I have to write about him.

If anyone asks me which snake I like the best, for looks, habits, friendliness, I'd surely vote for the Boa. This particular specimen is a Red-tailed Boa *Boa constrictor constrictor* from South America. The Boa is one of the largest American snakes; there have been specimens found up to eighteen feet long. This one is six feet long. It's tan with a rusty reddish tip on its tail and dark brown and lighter tan markings all over. The Huichol Indians of Mexico think it has some special power because of its beauty. Before a Huichol woman begins to weave, her husband catches a boa and the woman pats the snake. Then with the same hand she rubs her forehead and eyes. This is supposed to give her power to work beautiful patterns like the markings on the serpent's back.

I let Boa come out of his tank and wander around in my room when I have the door closed. Buzz got him used to being free and he seems to take it all

rather calmly. When he comes out, he usually crawls up the side of my desk and sits in the bookcase above my head, staring down at me with those big amber eyes of his. Sometimes he'll curl up on the window seat in the sun, half under the pillows. The first time Mom saw him there she was surprised, but now she's used to it, and will dust around him and plump up the pillows without batting an eye. I do think my mother is getting to be a genuine "herp."

I took Boa for a walk the other day. I just draped him around my neck and we strolled down the street. One of the kids asked me wasn't I afraid that he'd squeeze me to death. I explained that first of all he isn't big enough, and, secondly, a snake like a Boa would only constrict because he was afraid or hungry, and he was neither. I notice that Shalom is bitterly jealous of the snake. He slunk along with his head down all the time we were snake-walking. There's certainly no love lost between those two.

I believe Boa is sizing Shalom up as a potential meal, and I think Shalom knows it. Could a six-foot Boa eat a sixty-pound dog? Not a chance. But he sure has Shalom worried.

All I think about is food. Not for me. For the snakes. **July 17** Supplying food for my reptile brood is my chief occupation. Sometimes I wish that snakes were vegetarians. Right now we have more vegetables in our garden than we can possibly eat, so if the snakes ate greens we could grow them as much as they need. But of course snakes are *carnivores* (meat-eaters). And that's what makes my life so complicated.

Water Snake and Garter Snake are no problem. Sometimes I give them toads and frogs. They both eat fish, so I get scraps from the fish market once a week to keep them happy. I don't get only the flesh, either. I get gutsy parts, like the liver and other organs, which Mom, my nutrition advisor, says are the healthiest. It must be true because both snakes are doing well.

DeKay eats worms, and he's satisfied on a couple a week.

I gave up on the Hognose Snake. Even after he shed he wouldn't eat, so we finally let him go, up near where we'd found him. Buzz always said there's no sense in keeping a snake that doesn't eat.

The constrictors—Boa, Milk Snake, and the two Kingsnakes, are my biggest problems. They like rodents. *Like* is hardly the word. The first time I put a mouse in Milk Snake's tank, he gave us the classic example of how a constrictor works. As soon as I put the mouse in, his head came up. He began to stick his tongue out, "tasting" the air. Then he saw the mouse, and a second later, he struck. He coiled around it so fast that we could hardly see it happen. A few seconds later the mouse was dead, suffocated. As soon as it was still, the Milk Snake nudged it around until he was head to head with it. Then he started eating. Watching the process was pretty interesting, and Tim has a scheme to earn a new bike by charging admission to the kids in the neighborhood who want to see the constrictors eat.

Kingsnake, who's also a constrictor, goes about it pretty much the same way. The only difference is he's bigger, and it doesn't take as long a time for him to get a mouse down. He could probably eat a rat or a chipmunk, if I had one. He can eat a mouse in five minutes, until all you can see is the bulge in his belly.

Boa is the biggest eater. Or maybe I should say he eats the largest things. He downed a dead squirrel the first day I had him. He looked so funny with just the tail sticking out of his mouth—like a snake with a fur tongue!

I've discovered that if I bait a mousetrap with cheese and leave it in the garage, I catch a mole or a mouse every few days.

July 18

A SNAKE-LOVER'S DIARY

July 19 The mouse and mole supply is running out. Went to the pet store and *bought* a mouse. Expensive!

July 20 I'm trying something new. Buzz once suggested it to me. I'm going to *raise* mice to feed the snakes. I bought a female and a male mouse in the pet store. One of them is a really cute little tan guy. I've put them together in a cage in the basement. Time will tell.

July 21 Tim and I made some signs and circulated them in the neighborhood, much to Mom's embarrassment. They say, "Do you have a cat who brings home mice? Moles? Birds? Let us take them off your hands. Free pick-up service, if they are *freshly* dead." It's working.

I'm making an effort to lay in a supply of Boa food for the winter. I know that there won't be as many mice and moles around, and I *won't* shoot a bird, so I've sent my scouts (the kids in the neighborhood) to pass the word and to look for food on their bikes. So far our organization has produced the following: one Starling, killed by a cat; one squirrel, hit by a car; a Sparrow, killed flying into a glass window; and a beautiful Cardinal (cause of death unknown). We gave one to Boa and I have wrapped the rest carefully in aluminum foil and put them in the freezer. Mom says she still can't get used to having the snake's dinner and ours lying side by side in the same freezer.

Never feed two Kingsnakes together! That's what I discovered today, after a gruesome hour-long battle between me and the Kings.

Here's the way it went: I was cleaning one Kingsnake tank, so I put the two of them together. Everything seemed fine; they hardly paid attention to each other. I decided to feed them together, and, without thinking particularly, I put two mice in the tank. Each snake made a lunge for a mouse, and constricted it. Satisfied that both parties were having a good meal, I went back to my cleaning chore. A few minutes later I looked up and saw one Kingsnake in the process of swallowing the other one! He had the snake's head in his mouth and was gulping away for dear life.

I tried to pull the victim out of the other snake's jaws but they were both fighting mad. Something seems to happen to snakes when they eat. It's as if in the act of eating, a kind of over-all eating mechanism is triggered, and every *part* of the snake concentrates on it.

Anyway, I was in a spot. Two big snakes "locked in mortal combat," as they say in books, and nothing

A SNAKE-LOVER'S DIARY

Eastern Kingsnake

Florida Kingsnake

to pull them apart with. I looked around in desperation and spied my drum sticks sitting on the dresser. I grabbed them and began to dig into the knot of snakes to try and disentangle them. I felt as if I were trying to pick up a plateful of giant spaghetti with a set of chopsticks.

Finally I got them separated and they calmed down. When the family came home I told them what had happened. Mom promptly named them Hannibal and Cannibal. I'll *never* feed those two snakes in the same tank again.

5. August: Every little Movement

Yesterday I found four eggs in a hillside down at **July 30** Sand Dunes. They're certainly not birds' eggs. Too soft. Like Ping-Pong balls that have got a little waterlogged. And I'm pretty sure they're not snake eggs. I could almost bet they're turtle eggs. Too bad Buzz isn't here to consult with.

Anyway, I've brought them home. I put them in a big flowerpot full of sand. I didn't know whether I should put them close to the surface so they could get warmth from the sun, or deeper so they'd stay cool. So I put them at four different depths. That way I figure at least *one* will be right. I'm going to leave the pot in the den by the window, where Mom keeps her plants. I'll put a sign on them, so no one will plant flowers in that pot by mistake.

July 31   I've been doing some reading about eggs. An egg is a pretty wonderful thing, when you get to thinking about it. There it is, a perfect small "home" for an embryo to grow in. All the food inside to nourish it, a sac to take care of wastes, blood vessels to pick up oxygen, and a firm enough shell to keep out small animals, but still let air in.

   I just found out we have the reptiles to thank for the shelled egg. In fact, reptile eggs and reptiles developed at the same time, and the egg they evolved was such a good design that it has been in use, with very little change, ever since. Funny to think that we owe scrambled eggs to some ancient reptile.

August 1   Nothing much to do for the eggs now but wait. Meanwhile, we (Tim and I) are proceeding with our private investigation of snake locomotion. Today was a nice hot day for the experiment. So we took Boa and Garter Snake out on the front lawn. This immediately attracted a large crowd. In about ten minutes we had a dozen kids, the United Parcel driver, the mailman, and the collie from next door. I noticed something about that group. The little kids were a lot more willing to get close to the snakes than the grown-ups were. (Or the collie, for that matter.) Question: Is the fear of snakes something you're born with or something you learn?

The purpose of our gathering on the lawn was to observe the differences in the way snakes move. So Tim and I each released a snake onto the grass. Neither of them moved for a minute. Each one flicked out his tongue to get his bearings. Then they both started to move. Garter moved quickly, wriggling back and forth through the grass so fast that Tim had a hard time keeping an eye on him. Garter was using the "serpentine" motion, that is, pulling himself along by wrapping himself around small clumps of grass and pushing off from one to the other.

Then Boa started to move. But he didn't wriggle back and forth. He glided straight forward. The thick scales on the underside of his belly were moving and gripping, like the treads on a tank. This is called the "caterpillar" movement. A third move-

ment is like an accordion. The snake pulls itself together in a series of curves and then, by suddenly straightening out, manages to push forward. And if we'd had a Sidewinder Rattlesnake out there on the lawn, we'd have seen a fourth pattern of movement, sideways. Some snakes use only one type of movement, others use a combination. The audience was pretty impressed with the snakes' speed. One little kid said, "And they don't even have legs!"

I had to point out that the way a snake is built and moves does have some disadvantages. If he wants to move backwards he's out of luck; he has to turn all the way around to go the other way. The other thing is that many snakes can't move on a perfectly flat surface. If I put Garter on a pane of glass he couldn't move at all. Nothing to grab onto.

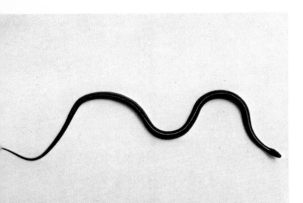

About this time our experiment got out of hand. Garter took off in one direction and Boa in the other. The crowd scattered and by the time we rounded up our wandering snakes we were happy to put them back in their tanks. I had really hoped to time them —see how fast they move and compare their rates of speed. I'll have to leave that for another time. I do know that a snake can't move as fast as a person, which seems to be a great comfort to the grown-ups in our neighborhood.

It rained today, so I watered the eggs. I decided that they would have gotten wet in their natural state, and I'm trying to duplicate natural conditions as much as possible. Nothing seems to be happening, but it's only a week.

August 6

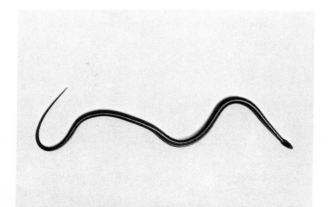

A SNAKE-LOVER'S DIARY

August 7 The Florida Kingsnake got out today. Again. That makes the third time. I must fix the top of that tank. The first time we found him in a closet in Dad's shoe. The second time he slithered into the studio while Dad was talking to a client. And now—

The first I knew about it was when Mom came storming into my room and said, "One of your *serpents* just crawled over my bare feet." It seems that King had got out of the tank in my room, and slithered right over her sandals as she stood at the kitchen sink. I asked her where he'd gone and she said behind the dishwasher.

I got the flashlight and looked in back there, but I couldn't see anything. So I shut off the water, undid the plumbing connections, and we pulled the dishwasher out from the wall. No snake. We finally decided that if he wasn't there he must be *in* the dishwasher. We unloaded all the dishes and tipped the dishwasher over on its side, but all we got was about a gallon of water all over the floor.

While Mom was mopping the floor, I got on my hands and knees and tried to look up into the works. Just then Dad appeared. When we told him what had happened he joined me on the floor and we both peered up into the dark depths of the dishwasher Finally, we spotted King—way up there in the warm coils, looking out at us with those steady unblinking eyes of his. Dad started to grin. When Mom asked him what was so funny he said he thought we ought to call the dishwasher repair service. He said he'd give anything to see the repair man's face when he discovered a snake in the dishwasher!

Mom and I were in no mood for practical jokes. We both wanted that snake out of there. So we decided to try to lure King out with something to eat. I got a mouse from my basement breeding cages and we put it on the floor in front of the dishwasher, under a strainer. Then we sat down to watch. Pretty soon King's head appeared at the end of the dishwasher and he began to wriggle out. He'd gotten the news of that mouse all the way up in his hideout. He came closer and closer, until all three and a half feet of him was out. When he lunged for the mouse, I grabbed him, put him back in his tank, and secured the top with a nice fat rock.

I gave him the mouse.

I wonder if and when the eggs are going to hatch. **August 10**

6. A Birth and a Death

Everybody in the family is waiting for the eggs to hatch. My father goes into the den about six times a day to take a look. Mom looks. Timmy looks. We're all like anxious parents.

August 14

August is too hot for collecting during the day. Nothing to do but bring my snake notebooks up to date. I've started a new system—a page for each snake. On it I write where I got the specimen, the date, the circumstances (under a log, on the highway, etc.), the time of day, and the size and condition of the specimen when I got it. Then I keep a record of when and what it eats, when it has a bowel movement, when it sheds, and any detail of its be-

August 20

havior that is interesting. That way, by glancing at the page, I get a sort of life history of that specimen, at least for the time I have it in my collection.

August 21 Early this evening I went into the den to check the eggs for the umpteenth time, and I noticed that the sand was disturbed. When I looked closely I saw a little brown bug sticking out of the sand. Then I looked more carefully and I saw that it wasn't a bug. It was a foot!

Everyone came running in when they heard me yell. We carried the bowl inside and put it on the kitchen table so we could watch. Then we cleared away some of the sand so we could see all of the eggs. Then we just waited. All of the eggs were cracked by this time. But only one of them had a foot waving out of it. And of course once we'd seen that scaly foot we *knew* for sure what was inside the eggs. Turtles!

The first one to hatch was the one nearest to the top of the bowl. (I wonder if warmth had something to do with it?) It took him about a half hour. He had already broken through the shell when we first saw him, and so we could only guess that he had made the first break with his *shell-breaker,* that temporary egg tooth at the end of his beak.

As soon as he staggered out onto the sand, I knew what kind of turtle we'd hatched in our den. The conversation went something like this:

Me: "It's a Painted Turtle!"

They: "How do you know?"

"Look at the red and black on its *carapace.*"

"Its what?"

"Carapace. The top shell."

We looked him over. His head was brown, and along each side of his neck were two bright yellow dots. His carapace was decorated with red and black markings.

I picked him up and turned him over. I showed Mom and Dad and Tim the yellow food sac on his *plastron,* or bottom shell. "Looks like his belly button," was Tim's comment. They just couldn't believe that it was the turtle's food supply.

I explained how the turtle absorbs food from this little "button" until he's ready to go to the water and look for his own food. The Eastern Painted

Turtle *Chrysemys picta picta* is among the most aquatic of turtles, and it doesn't move too far away from the water except when it lays its eggs. So the babies have a built-in lunch box until they can get back to their natural source of food. Remarkable, Dad says.

Within two hours we had four baby Painted Turtles swimming around in a big dishpan. We put a rock island in the middle for them to climb out on, and, satisfied that we had our nursery well set up, we went to bed.

I feel like a real hero. Those turtles would never have survived lying out in the hot sun on that hillside. Some people might say "so what," but I'm glad my family thinks turtles are important.

August 22   Tim just can't believe turtles are reptiles. "But they're so *different* from snakes," he keeps saying.

"Think about the rules," I reminded him. "Reptiles are cold-blooded vertebrates that have scales, shields or plates, their toes have claws, and the newborn young are replicas of their parents."

In a few days I'm going to start feeding the baby turtles bugs and pieces of earthworm. And then, after I've taken pictures of them and observed them for a while, I'll let them go.

August 23

Boa seems rather quiet lately. He doesn't come out of his tank even when I have the cover off. Maybe he's going to shed, although his eyes aren't cloudy.

August 25

Something is wrong with Boa. He's not eating, and he's always had a good appetite. I wish I knew more about snake diseases. Could he possibly have a cold? I know snakes get tiny bugs, called mites, on their scales. I thought that's what it might be, so I put him in the bathtub and let him swim around for a while. Then I dried him off. But I didn't see any mites, either on him or in the water. It can't be that. I wish Buzz were here.

August 26

I tried to force-feed Boa today. I opened his jaws with one of those tongue depressors that doctors use to look down a person's throat. I was going to push a piece of lamb down. But as soon as I saw the inside of his mouth I stopped. Whatever is wrong with Boa is in his mouth. His gums are swollen and raw-looking and there's an odd white cheesy-looking deposit around some of his teeth. No wonder he can't eat, poor fellow. I can't wait for Buzz to come home.

August 28 Buzz is home, and has given me the bad news. Boa has mouthrot, and it's going to kill him. If I had known what it was, I might have been able to cure it by washing his mouth out with disinfectant. But now Buzz says it has reached the bone, and it's too late.

A BIRTH AND A DEATH

If anyone else asks me, "Can you really get attached to a snake?" I am going to punch him right in the nose. The answer is yes! yes! yes!

No more quiet companion on the window seat. No more amber eyes looking at me from the bookcase. Boa died this morning.

August 30

Buzz said he'd show me how to preserve him, the way they do in the museum. But somehow I didn't want to. I took him out and buried him under the big ash tree. I didn't make a big thing of it. Just buried him. And that's that. I'll have to get used to some of my specimens dying if I want to be a scientist. But nobody knows how bad I feel about Boa.

7. September: An Ending

Today is the beginning of a new month. It also marks the end of my summer of collecting. Today I released all four of the baby Painted Turtles, the Garter Snake, the Water Snake, the DeKay's Snake, and the Milk Snake. All I have left are the Kingsnakes.

I could have kept the collection over the winter. I could have kept them warm with heat lights above the tanks, and fed them fish parts and mice the way I've been doing. But I think it's better for them to hibernate in their natural way, and next spring I can collect new specimens. Timmy says he guesses they'll be happier in their freedom. I'm not so sure that a snake feels happiness, but they'll almost certainly be healthier hibernating in their normal way.

A SNAKE-LOVER'S DIARY

The whole family (including Shalom) made the pilgrimage. We deposited each reptile where I'd originally caught it. I released Garter Snake in the field. I let Water Snake go at the riverbank, right near the log where I first saw him. We let DeKay go near the tennis court and we put the Milk Snake in the woods near where the metal sign was.

We let the turtles go in the water below the hillside where I had found the eggs. But first we marked them. We painted a small circle on each turtle's carapace with thick acrylic paint. "Now they're really 'painted' turtles," was Tim's comment. Next spring, when we come down to the Forty-Foot Hole, we'll have a way of identifying "our" Painted Turtles if we should see one.

What's left in the collection? Just the Kingsnakes. I can't release them, because they don't come from around here. Besides, I *think* they're male and female, and I'd like to try to breed them, if it's possible to breed two different subspecies. (Buzz says it is.) Mom says she hopes Hannibal won't eat Cannibal instead of mating with her. We'll see.

September 2

Tomorrow school starts. Part of me is looking forward to it, but part of me hates to see the summer end. I guess you could say that this is the summer I became a "herp." In fact, the whole family have become herps. We've all learned a lot. And yet we've hardly scratched the surface.

We're already making plans for next spring. Next spring I'm going to raise some frogs from tadpoles. Next spring we're going to build an outdoor turtle pen. Next spring I'm going to catch newts and salamanders and study that form of amphibian life.

And lizards. I wonder how many different kinds of lizards live around here? How come lizards can drop their tails and grow new ones? Next year I'm going to devote myself to studying lizards. Even their names make you want to learn more about them —Horned Lizard, Spiny Lizard, Collared Lizard, Earless Lizard, Iguana. . . .

I think I'll buy Mom an Iguana for Christmas.

GLOSSARY OF WORD MEANINGS

AMPHIBIAN—*any animal of the class Amphibia.*

AQUATIC—*living or growing in water.*

CARAPACE—*the top shell of a turtle.*

CARNIVORE—*meat-eater.*

CARUNCLE—*the temporary horny projection on the snout of baby turtles, used to break out of the eggshell.*

CLOACA—*digestive and reproductive canal of a snake.*

CONSTRICTOR—*snake which squeezes its prey in its coils.*

EMBRYO—*an organism in the earliest stages of its development.*

ENVIRONMENT—*total surroundings, conditions, and influences.*

EVOLUTION—*adaptation of organisms to environment by genetic change.*

GRAVID—*bearing eggs or young.*

HEMIPENES—*pair of tubelike structures that are the sex organs of male snakes.*

HERPETOLOGIST—*a zoologist who specializes in the study of reptiles and amphibians.*

HIBERNATE—*to spend a period of time in a dormant condition.*

JACOBSEN'S ORGAN—*a sensory organ of snakes, located in the mouth.*

MITES—*small parasites which may affect certain reptiles.*

ORGANISM—*any form of animal or plant life.*

PIT VIPER—*a venomous snake which has heat-sensing pits on each side of its head.*

PLASTRON—*bottom shell of a turtle.*

REPTILE—*a class of cold-blooded vertebrates having scales, shields or plates, and whose toes have claws.*

RODENT—*animal belonging to the order Rodentia, having teeth especially adapted for gnawing. Includes mice, squirrels, beavers, rats, etc.*

SCALES—*the thin, flat plate coverings of snakes.*

SHEDDING—*process by which snakes and some other reptiles replace their outer layer of skin.*

SPECIES—*a group of animals or plants that have certain permanent characteristics in common which distinguish them from all other organisms.*

SPECIMEN—*one of a group or class taken to show what others are like; single part, thing, etc. regarded as an example of its kind, or a single example, typical of its group or class.*

VENOM—*a poisonous fluid secreted by some reptiles.*

VENOMOUS—*secreting venom.*

SOME OTHER BOOKS ABOUT REPTILES

Carr, Archie, THE REPTILES. (Life Nature Library.) New York: Time, Inc.

Conant, Roger, A FIELD GUIDE TO REPTILES AND AMPHIBIANS. Boston: Houghton, Mifflin Co., 1958.

Kauffeld, Carl, SNAKES AND SNAKE HUNTING. Garden City, N.Y.: Hanover House.

———, SNAKES: THE KEEPER AND THE KEPT. New York: Doubleday, 1969.

Pope, Clifford H., SNAKES ALIVE AND HOW THEY LIVE. New York: Viking Press, 1937.

Schmidt, Karl, and Inger, Robert, LIVING REPTILES OF THE WORLD. New York: Doubleday & Co., Inc., 1957.

HERPETOLOGICAL ORGANIZATIONS

New York Herpetological Society
P.O. Box 27
West Farms Station
Bronx, N.Y. 10460

Herpetologists League
Secretary Frederick B. Turner
Laboratory of Nuclear Medicine and Radiation Biology
University of California
Los Angeles, Calif. 90024

American Society of Ichthyologists and Herpetologists
Division of Reptiles and Amphibians
United States National Museum
Washington, D.C. 20560

Society for Study of Amphibians and Reptiles
Secretary Joseph Collins
Museum of National History
University of Kansas
Lawrence, Kansas 66044

PICTURE CREDITS